Going In With Flowers

Avril Joy

Published by Linen Press, London 2019
8 Maltings Lodge
Corney Reach Way
London
W4 2TT

www.linen-press.com

© 2019 Avril Joy

The right of Avril Joy to be identified as the author of this work has been asserted by her in accordance with the Copyright, Designs and Patents Act 1988.

The names of all the people in the poems and prose pieces have been changed to protect their identities.

All rights reserved. This book is sold subject to the condition that it shall not, by way of trade or otherwise, be lent, resold, hired out, or otherwise circulated without the publisher's prior consent in any form of binding or cover other than that in which it is published and without a similar condition, including this condition, being imposed on the subsequent purchaser.

A CIP catalogue record for this book is available from the British Library.

Cover image: Unsplash – Alex Loup
Typeset by Zebedee Design.
Printed and bound by Lightning Source
ISBN 978-1-9996046-0-8

About Avril Joy

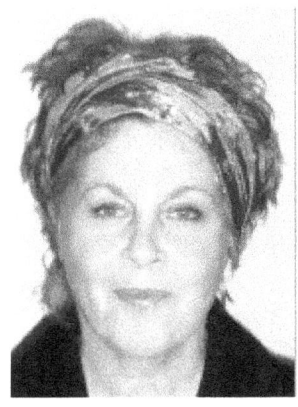

Before becoming a full-time writer, Avril Joy worked for twenty-five years in Low Newton women's prison in County Durham. Her short fiction has appeared in literary magazines and anthologies including Victoria Hislop's, *The Story: Love, Loss & the Lives of Women*. Her work has been shortlisted in competitions including the Bridport, the Manchester Prize for Fiction and the Raymond Carver Short Story Prize. In 2012 her story, *Millie and Bird*, won the inaugural Costa Short Story Award.

Her novel, *Sometimes a River Song*, published by Linen Press, won the 2017 People's Book Prize for outstanding achievement. Her poetry has appeared both in print and online. In 2019 her poem *Skomm* won the York Literary Festival poetry competition. Avril lives with her partner near Bishop Auckland, in County Durham and posts regularly at www.avriljoy.com

Other Books by Avril Joy

Sometimes a River Song – Linen Press 2016

Millie and Bird, Tales of Paradise – Iron Press 2015

From Writing With Love – 2013

The Sweet Track – Flambard Press 2007

For women in prison everywhere

*There are always flowers for those
who want to see them.*
Henri Matisse

Acknowledgements

Acknowledgements are due to the editors of *Ink, Sweat and Tears, Strix, Algebra of Owls, Snakeskin, Atrium, Dreamcatcher and Brittle Star* where some of these poems first appeared.

Skomm won first prize in the York Literary Festival/York Mix 2019 competition, judged by Clare Shaw. *Doing Money* was commended in the same competition.

Thanks are due to Carole Bromley and Kate Clanchy for being inspirational Arvon tutors and for making me believe this project was possible.

Also to my editor, Lynn Michell for her friendship, her unstinting support and her editorial skills. Thank you, Lynn, for always helping to make the book the best it can be. Huge thanks also to Federica, Nam, Hannah and Jen, the lovely Linen Press interns, for their enthusiasm and hard work.

As always thanks are due to my friend and mentor, writer, Wendy Robertson, who lives alongside me through every book, and who worked with me in the prison.

Finally, thank you to my family for their enduring love and support. A special thank you to my father, Patrick, who sadly did not live to see this book published but who always believed in me and took pride in what I did.

Contents

SHAME	13
Skomm	20
What I Know	22
Peace – Lily	24
Skin	26
Anemone	28
Lapidation	29
Blindsimmer	31
Aztec Love Song for Women in Prison	33
If I'd smuggled you through the Search Tank, past the dogs	34
I Stayed Put	35
SANCTUARY	39
Garden Escapee	45
Keep a Green Tree in Your Heart and a Singing Bird Will Come	47
Classroom	49
Prayer for the Out	50
The Comfort of Women	52
Fight	54
The Listening Project	56
Tulip Fever	57

Asylum   58

SILENCE   63
The Fifth Labour   71
Mary Oliver Says – You do not have to be good   72
We Are All Made of Stars   74
At the inquest   75
In a Painting by Vermeer   76
Infanticide   78
In the Segregation Unit   83
Stone Dress   85
Agnes Richter's jacket   87

WINDOWS AND GATES   89
Going in With Flowers   97
What Men Do   99
How to Spend Twenty-Five Years Inside   101
Meeting on the Wing   103
Hysteria   104

VOICES   107
Rain   114
The Karaoke Queen's survival kit   116
Pig-Girl   117
H.R.H.   119
Doing Money   121
What I Did in the Summer Holidays   123
Bombing   125
Sheree   127

Fire	128
Remedy for a Small Voice	130
Letter to a Prisoner	131
Duty Governor	133
Key Pouch and Belt	134
LEAVING	135
My Mother the Owl	140
And Ghosts Return Gently at Twilight	142
On a Summer Evening	143
In the Night Garden	144
Sky Glow	146
All That's Needed Are Sunglasses	148
The temple bell stops but I still hear the sound coming out of the flowers – Basho	149

SHAME

Shame

Even though it's more than ten years since I set foot inside Low Newton, I still dream about prison. Mostly I dream about the people I worked with there and not the place. I don't dream of iron gates, double-locked, painted cream, scratched, blistering, worn back to the metal with the relentless pushing of feet. I don't hear them clanged shut, or that everyday percussion of keys in a lock. That my dreams are not full of the bricks and mortar is less surprising when I remember how easily I entered in the first place; how little the architecture and paraphernalia of prison bothered me. How quickly it became a part of my daily life.

It bothered some people greatly. I met teachers who would come for interview and declare immediately that the job was not for them. They could not imagine coming through the prison gates ever again. But for the most part, I never minded going in. What I did mind, in the early days especially, was the reception that I knew was waiting for me, when having entered through the gatehouse and crossed the yard, I found myself in front of the doors of the old Female Wing. I minded then. I want to say it felt like standing at the gates of Hell, but that would probably be an exaggeration – the entrance to Hades perhaps? I look back and wonder how I did it. How I ran the gauntlet of that Wing to reach my classroom.

Built around a small quadrangle of rough grass, with a rowan tree at it centre, the Wing was claustrophobic and highly controlled. Staffed by women only, its regime was rigid and lacked compassion. Female prisoners were considered to be sub-human and even the teachers who worked in the main jail, which was a Remand Centre for men under twenty-one, refused to teach in the Female Wing. It was a bleak, unhappy place, full – as prisons are – of shame and secrets. It was a place where secrets were kept; a place where secrets were spilled. The most shameful of these were like wounds.

It is hard for a woman, in the small, cramped dark of a cell to keep the secret she's been hiding even from herself. It may well visit her there in her flashbacks and nightmares. Alone, she is forced to confront the guilt and shame she feels for being in prison at all; for her crime, for what she's done, for the way society condemns her, for her failure as a woman, as a mother. In my experience, women in prison are deeply ashamed of where they are and what they've become.

Outside, holding on to secrets had kept them safe. But in the crisis of coming into prison, with everything splintered and lost, the truth threatened to devour them. The things that never should have happened were laid bare before their eyes. Their secrets infected them like a plague and they feared if you knew them, really knew them, then you would abandon them in disgust.

The worst of these secrets, the longest held and the deepest, was the cause of their *Skomm*, their shame, the goose on the head: the hidden secrets of childhood. Prison was often a catalyst in bringing these secrets to the surface. Sometimes when the light crept in, when a good officer sat on a prisoner's bed to offer comfort, when a teacher in the classroom or a chaplain in the chapel paid attention, the secret was revealed. I hold some of these secrets still, after many years, and have told no one. They are nearly all secrets of abuse. Of sexual abuse.

Often the horror of these disclosures lay in the small, almost inconsequential, details that even now I struggle to forget. It's not that I would ask. It's that once trust was built, the women found ways of telling. In those early days of teaching – the days when paper was rationed with every page in every exercise book numbered by a prisoner whose job it was – I would quietly defy the regime by freely giving out unnumbered pages. To be without pen and paper seemed to me to be a breach of human rights that I wasn't willing to be party to and somehow I got away with it. The result was that many women who took paper from me would return to my classroom door with their life stories for me to read. They wrote their shame and their secrets on the page, just as they wrote them on their bodies.

The marks of self-harm are always evident in a women's prison and often alarming: cutting with razors or broken biro casings, the inserting of numerous small objects, like staples and pins, grazing with scotch pads, blood letting, ligature marks. Skin that hangs loose like cloth, like crepe paper. Skin so bad, so red raw, so bloody you hardly dare look. Skin wrapped in so many layers of clothing it's hard to see the person beneath. All, ways of coping, all, marks of shame. Of what the world has done to the women.

Added to this was my own shame. The shame I felt at the way we incarcerated and still do incarcerate, the women most in need of our care. Walking through the corridors of a women's prison you could be forgiven for thinking you were in a psychiatric hospital. The women we lock up are themselves victims of the worst crimes. I tried to speak up about this many times, and in many ways, including outside of the prison, in conference halls and in the media, but to no avail. Perhaps we weren't ready to hear it. In the 1980s and 90s abuse was still a well-kept secret and there were many who preferred it that way. Those of us who did speak up were branded as dangerous and ultimately silenced.

When the prison re-roled to become a women's prison, I had the opportunity to work with an enlightened Governor and a Senior Officer, training wing staff in how to cope with disclosures from the women which they were finding very difficult. Together we wrote a course which we began to deliver at Low Newton and which soon became respected and known so that we received requests for the training from prisons all over the country.

The Area Manager, however, was not happy. He accused us, in writing, of being dangerous and of working beyond our remit. We were ordered to stop immediately. It didn't seem to matter that I'd undertaken specialist training or that staff said it was the best, most relevant training they'd ever had, or that the Inspectorate had singled out our work as an example of good practice. The origins of shame had reared their ugly heads and had to be buried again, as Jung observed, to 'eat away at the soul.' Eat away at my soul it did, for a good while. It's hard to be accused of something when you believe yourself to be innocent. But ultimately it didn't eat away at my soul in the way that the shame which haunts every woman in prison eats away at hers.

The power of shame lies in its imposition and in the silence of not being able to speak out. Prison is by its nature a closed institution where power often lies in the hands of a few. For prisoners and many staff it can be difficult to speak out. Prison is a power play, and there will always be those who enjoy the power of imposing and withholding, who enjoy the secrecy and the silencing.

But prison is also a place full of contradictions and there were many people, good people, who cared and worked hard to make the prison a better place. Without them, it would not have been possible to stay.

Skomm

Skomm is an old Norse word meaning shame

The girl with the goose on her head sits
by the window in the corner of the classroom,
there are others with her, among them
her sister, their geese barely a wing less visible.
The weight of goose swells the air, the room is ripe
with the scent of goose shit.
I put down my bag, take off my scarf and coat
and wonder about the snow covering the road.
Outside the wind is up and the yard is frosting over.
Better make a start, I say. They pick up pens, open
books. The girl with the goose on her head declines
to write, says she cannot concentrate for the load,
the poundage, shortened neck, compacted spine,
for centuries of carrying: *scamu, skomm,* shame,
the bird force fed, gavage-pipe in the oesophagus,
on its back, legs splayed, neck craned, half-buried
in its chest, the words whispered in a father's bed.
She says she cannot stop thinking, *None of us can,
the nights are the worst,*
corralled, wings beating, they leave their bodies,
fly up in a blizzard, a captive murmuration.
*Jesus, look at the snow. Will you get home alright
Miss? What about the kids?*
I look out at the fattening flakes, the absent ground.

I taste the goose
all twenty pounds of it, sweat and stink.
Snow falls on my tongue the lightest it's been.
I'll get home alright, I say, *now close your books.*
What will it be?
A story, say the girls with geese,
and they fold their arms, lay down their heads.

What I Know

Every afternoon I cross the yard to gates, locked
doors, press the bell and wait, without keys,
not knowing for how long.
What I already know: this, me, I am not a priority.
If the bell is answered
it will most likely be by chance.
To press twice is severely frowned on.
Whenever the gate is opened I will smile
as if I mean it, big time.
I will be greeted like an unwanted salesman on a job
creation scheme, selling dusters and dishcloths.
It will be my smile that gets me in.
They consider me harmless.
I am a hypocrite. Hypocrisy my survival.
I will go to the P.O.'s office to collect the classroom
cupboard keys, and talk about holidays, caravans
and nails. Only later, much later, will she tell me
how her son left her.
She will smoke and smile like an assassin.
Without fail an officer will find a new way
to tell me theirs is the worst of all worlds.
Without fail someone will call the prisoners
little liars, little shits, scum bags.
It is only a short walk from the P.O.s office
to A Wing, if the gates are unlocked.
The wing will smell of fags and bleach.

The cell doors are blue.
Someone will be on her bell being ignored.
In the S.O.s office they will be drinking tea.
Somewhere an officer will be shouting at a spy flap
winding a prisoner up.
If I were braver I would call it all out,
if I were braver I'd be locked out.
You are waiting in our classroom
no bigger than a cupboard.
When I get there it will feel like home.

Peace – Lily

Not what you're wearing: these jungle fatigues, green and black,
a dense and tangled vegetation, tree frog, jaguar disguise.

Not the smell of you: feral, musk, your own eco system
moist under the canopy of clothes:
hats – two, woollen and camouflage
underwear – doubled up
trousers – leggings and combats
vest tops – two
shirt – one, lumberjack
jumper – two, plus hoodie
body warmer – on top quilted
socks – to the knees several
boots – heavy duty military
coats – two, relinquished in Reception – padded with zips

Not this inventory, excess of drapery, not the skin beneath
unwashed and bloodied, hatched in your fascination for sharp objects,
not the rollie you're smoking damp as tobacco leaf lips.
Not the what of buttressed roots, but the why.
A matter of Health and Safety; this armouring, this

undergrowth
not easily penetrated, delaying tactic
for hand to hand combat, Venus fly trap of fabric.

Not the what but the way we meet as old friends,
as if on a familiar street corner. Your wry smile
when I do as they ask and try to persuade you
that a bath is a good idea.
The small shake of your head
that declines, your fringe loosened, epiphyte,
pale face tilted as you look up at me,
peace-lily in the dark understory of the rainforest.

Skin

this grey
this yellow
this hep
this no vein left
vampire sucked
steel-sink washed
laid out fluorescent strip
this creased
this pleated
this crepe paper garland
limp in heat
this Nivea doused
canteen soaped
copper lit
gas of cabbage
this grazed net
bandaged and seeped
this aching to be touched
this violated
broken
excommunicated
this drawn on
discarded
crumpled in the bin
this red to bursting
gateway to splinter

this needle
this draining cup
this once tender
once infant
this once gave birth.

Anemone

You say it's graffitied on your forehead
there for everyone to see, written
large, your naked halo, tribal scarf,
snow of powdered glass, rodent
in your gut it's there neon and lit-up.
Abuse me, hollow, scar, maul and pluck
me, I'm up for it, can't you tell?
Have been since the words first appeared
there scrawled by uncles of men.

You say you are landfill, roadkill
left on the tarmac for the crows.
If only I could show you what else
cached behind the violet of your eyes,
silver mussel shell of oceanic memory
opening and closing with the tide
and you, anemone, flower of the sea
floating unharvested on the coral reef
milking your helpless prey.

Lapidation

I hear them calling – slag, slut, whore,
not fit to be a mother
keep her children,
not fit to be called woman.
Witch, monster, MILF, pedo sister
nympho, ugly fat bitch.

Don't you know women are discrete
not lumpen or obese?
Women don't eat.
Or shout rape.
Women don't bruise,
women don't bleed.

They stay indoors, are not trafficked
across continents, sold into slavery
prised open nightly
receptacle to be used

over
and over, and over.

Women are
not disproportionately
sentenced by the courts,
especially not for a first offence

or shoplifting, or depression
or blood letting

and as for #metoo
that's me not you,
women are not immune to the calling.
Bag, cow, cunt, minger,
jailbait, doxie, slattern, tart,
bimbo, ballbreaker, wifey, nag.

How to stop a woman sinning:
dig a neat hole in the ground
bind her arms to her body, lower her in,
provide rocks for the stoning.

Blindsimmer

A blindsimmer – one who desires and pretends to be visually impaired

Pigeons fly in and settle on the prison roof
your head drifts up like a little boat,

you take her arm, she guides you
round the quadrangle of bitten grass,

a girl in school, thin scholar of Braille
at home with the white stick.

What made you blindsimmer?
Was it the pit already dug behind your eyes

or the long since wish to be rid of vision,
all those half-looks, all your staring

at the sun, did he fail to understand
what brought the loss you craved?

Is that why you killed him?
A miracle that you stayed.

I imagine a quietness in blindsimmer,
like the faded print of an antique chintz,

despite the discord, despite the doctor's
clacking shoes on the corridor

the pigeons coo – cooing. Let her lead
you to the bench under the rowan,

sit among us, in this house what difference?
We are all simmers of one kind or another.

Sit under the rowan and wonder
how it might be to treesimmer, to suck

your nourishment from the earth and fall
into blossom and leaf with each new spring.

Aztec Love Song for Women in Prison

I carry them to your house on my back,
uprooted flowers.
I am bent double with the weight of them,
of women torn from the soil, their roots mud
stem and sepal crushed
I carry them.

I carry their scent, the scent of ash
and blood in my blood.
Bent double with the weight of their fragility,
buds unopened, roses full-blown
discarded, trampled on
I carry them.

Their flower faces sit, geranium,
harebell, meadow-sweet,
in my classroom,
foliage fluttering in the breeze
from a barely open window
I carry the leaf of them,

bent double with the weight
of what we do to them,
how we punish and incarcerate,
condemn to iron fallen blossom, uprooted
flowers I carry them
on my back, to your house.

If I'd smuggled you through the Search Tank, past the dogs

persuaded them, made them listen in their offices
and their conference halls
bought a bicycle and a Tanoy, made the streets ours.
If I'd taken up your letting cup,
tipped blood backwards to your veins
ironed your crumpled skin like a skirt smooth
at its seams, like a skirt for dancing in.
If I'd opened the prison gates and let them swing
torn down fences, dug tunnels like P.O.W.S.
If I'd given you a notebook of swanskin
embossed with your name,
if we'd sipped tea together from porcelain,
the space around us grown to cathedrals.
If I'd shown you the lacing pattern of leaves
the still pillow of night over hills,
bought the day like heroin and banished dreams,
if we'd eaten papaya and mango from the trees,
swum in the Indian ocean
thrown ourselves at waves resisting undertow.
If we'd stood on stilts like stilt fisherman,
like Jesus on his cross
guarding the lost children on the beach.
If I'd shown you how the world can sometimes be.

I Stayed Put

After Clare Shaw's, I Came Back

I stayed put; even
when they called me dangerous
I hung about, under cover of brick
the building held me.

I stuck it out
in the warehouse of grief, its boxes
sealed according to decree.
I befriended keys.

In the absence of roses
or laurel I stayed for the ease
of no day ever the same, the lists I made
each night before leaving,

I stayed for the keening
past the famine of numbered pages,
in exercise books, for lock down, hostage
prisoner on the roof,

rope at my neck
choking what mattered most,
I stayed for the mangoes.
For Father Danny's boiled sweets

the rice in the drains,
the walk-in fridge. I stayed for the dead.
I stayed for the dreaming,
for the rising of bones

for the insufficiency
of the poems we pinned on walls.
I stayed for the stories
we wrote, for the stories you told.

I stayed through thunder
winter, summer solstice,
the Orange Prize for Fiction reading group.
I stayed for the tea urn,

the green book, the tea set
we bought from a charity shop
and the t-bags we packed
in the packing lot.

I stayed
where imagination soared:
not every prison has a key
not every prisoner held.

I stayed because you called
to me from one end of the jail to another
because we lived in each other,
disputing disbelief.

I stayed for the leaves,
laughter, crack, backs to silver
the wind in the wire
the gates between worlds.

For Proteus
and the salvage of dreams,
acute sense of hearing
knife of obsidian

cutting through bells
the damp still of morning rain,
do you know who I am,
do you know why I stay?

I stayed for the meadow lark
timber yard, tidal pool
of my past, swimmer in the deep
diver on the reef

I stuck it out
the best of me and the worst,
I stayed because
you knew I wasn't dangerous.

SANCTUARY

Sanctuary

If I ever find myself in prison, on the wrong side of the law that is, the first thing I'll do is sign up for work in the gardens. I'll become one of the garden girls with their green uniforms and outdoor boots. Should you ever find yourself in prison, you'd be wise to follow my example.

As I write this, I'm looking out onto my own garden, at the blossom on the cherry tree, and thinking that no matter how fleeting, every year the blossom brings beauty and joy. It is restorative. Gardens are restorative, and prison gardens are no exception. Whenever I wanted to get away from the prison I would slip out of the doors at the back of the kitchen and go out to the gardens and greenhouses. Those were the only places where you could see the whole of the sky, taste the day, smell the slip from one season to another.

I liked to think of my classroom as a garden, as a place where it was possible to bloom, if only briefly. A place where a woman could find something good in the sanctuary of the prison, and in herself. When you're penniless, living on the street, or working on the street, addicted to drugs or alcohol, when you're up to your eyes in debt and living in fear of your partner and the machete he's got hidden under the bed, when you're caught in an endless cycle of abuse and domestic violence, when your life is broken into so many pieces it's impossible to fit them back together, then prison is not such a bad place to be.

For some women, many women, the prison was a breathing space, a safety-net, a place where they could get off the drugs at least for a while, feel safe, even perhaps dare to hope. They could find friendship and comfort among the other women. In prison, women could engage in meaningful work. In the classroom, they could even learn to read. Once the classroom door was closed, it was possible to create and inhabit a new world, a different world, apart. A sanctuary that was humane and respectful, serious but fun, relevant and equal. It was us, not me and them, and it was not so different from the teaching I'd done in schools. I was still *Miss* and the women in many ways were like my children. They were children in need of mothering. But they were mothers too and were always kind to me, worrying if I wasn't well or if I seemed tired or troubled.

In the classroom we talked about things that mattered: home, family, love, children, painful though it sometimes was. We read stories and poems, wrote some too, worked on basic skills in English and Maths, drew pictures, made collages, laughed, joked, occasionally cried and sometimes sang. I did my best to make it a creative and happy space for everyone. A hopeful place where women could retrieve something of their self-esteem. It didn't always work of course. There were times when a woman, determined to disrupt the peace, would haul her anger into the room and turn everything over like a storm. Times when women would pick on other women or on me. There were one or two fights along the way, but for the most part we lived in harmony, even if it was a noisy kind of harmony.

There were other places of sanctuary in the prison: the Library, the Learning Shop, the Chapel. Quiet or troubled women gravitated to the Art room where they could find expression without words, where they could concentrate on something outside of themselves, and outside of the prison, where they could work on paintings of landscapes, flowers, blossom…as gifts to send out when they had nothing else to give. If I ever found myself in prison, I'd join the Art class too.

When we could find the money, there were arts and music projects, and for several years there was our Writer in Residence who brought the gift of voice to the voiceless. Being given permission to write, to be creative, seeing their words on the page and in print was a unique and powerful experience for the women. As it was for me. I'd never considered myself good at writing. My schooling had led me to believe I couldn't write, at least not well. My work would often be covered with the dreaded red pen (I have never used one myself) highlighting my mistakes and my poor spelling. I'd written nothing since the poems of my childhood and I had no aspiration to be a writer until I met author Wendy Robertson, Low Newton's Writer in Residence. Only when I began working on projects with her did writing become inevitable. She told me I was a writer. Meeting Wendy transformed my life and led eventually to me leaving prison to write full-time. Such transformations are precious and rare, I think. I hope that along the way I too managed to inspire and to offer the women who came into my classroom the possibility of change.

I was told many times by prisoners about the sanctuary of the cell. Although at it worst the cell was a dangerous place, at its best it was the place, they said, where time passed quickest, where the prison mask was removed, and the imagination could find release. Being alone in your cell meant you could imagine yourself in another world entirely. This was freedom. Many women, especially in the days of the old Female Wing, said: 'They can take away my freedom, Miss, but not my mind.' Such assertions gave them comfort. It gave them mastery in a world of passivity. They knew the power of transcending the walls of their cell, of imagining a walk in a familiar place with a child by their side, her hand in theirs.

Prisoners everywhere across the world know the power of imagination. It's essential for their survival. I know this. I heard it first in prison but finding myself inexorably drawn to the writings of prisoners, I've also read about it many times. What the Turkish novelist, Ahmet Altan, imprisoned in his home country, has to say about the triumph of the spirit echoes the words of the women I knew. In his memoir, *I Will Never See the World Again*, Altan says, 'You can imprison me but you cannot keep me here… like all writers, I have magic… I can pass through your walls with ease.'

I'm happy and grateful to say I have no first-hand experience of being in a cell for any length of time but I was once locked in a cell with a prisoner by mistake. She was more scared, much more scared than me because while there was nothing for me to be scared about, she thought she would get the blame, even though it was the officer's fault. He'd shut and locked the cell door without looking. The prisoner pressed her emergency bell and shouted like crazy. The officer came back and unlocked the door. When he saw me and realised what he'd done, he turned very pale and very quiet. No doubt he was thinking how I might have been taken hostage, harmed, even killed, and it would have been down to him. Once he'd recovered, we went outside together for some air and a cigarette and I told him not to fret. But I teased him about it afterwards, every chance I got.

Garden Escapee

Inside
the greenhouse
gentle careful work,
wet earth.

Lemon geranium,
marigold, pricked out
pushed back
to compost.

Under the bench
terracotta pots
ghost ferns,
a toad in hiding.

On top
tea in a mug
that a spoon could
stand up in.

Cuttings
of stonecrop
for autumn
bedding,

soft-pedal radio
quelled boot leather
thickening
wool

sticky with lichen
ear to glass
hear the green
sigh

of the place
least like that
you seek
to escape.

Coming out,
on your shoes,
the scuffed petals
of a yellow rose.

Keep a Green Tree in Your Heart and a Singing Bird Will Come

I ask you to sing for me, sing for us, before the bell
to end morning class,

this might be the last time I see you – at least
for a while,

don't give your things away tonight I want to say,
don't tempt the fates.

Sing, back to radiator, bars and clouded pane,
indifferent day

what happens out there is nothing to do with us
but wind in leaf.

Sing, snatching time, bring us your small circuses
of hope, your caravans of desire.

Make fists of our hearts, anthologise our loss.
Stand in the ring,

roses at your feet and sing – the one – you know
where love comes in

and the flattened, stamped-on grass springs up
with sap

rousing sleeping lions to jump through fire.
Sing, love urgent

without appointment, bloom of coral, bee on
lavender, bruised lip. Sing,

transform our torn ballerina skirts and launch us
into the big-top

soft body of the universe, Lake of Forgetfulness,
Lake of Softness, Lake of Spring,

take the lid off, sing. Crack the silence, drown
prison's mute submission,

possess us with your longing 'til, green tree
in our hearts, we forget who we are.

Classroom

When the classroom picked itself up
and took us to the edge of the sea,
tipped us out in the sand and stole our shoes,
it was just us; it was just she:
she who didn't go to school past ten
she who stayed home to look after everyone;
mother to child, wife to father,
baby food and special brew,
a bottle of value vodka,
was something we knew about.
She who robbed the neighbours,
pimped her sister, sex-worker, slave,
she the peace protestor, grafter and fence,
council tax defaulter, illegal immigrant,
she complicit in a child's murder,
she the lifer who set fire to her abuser
– all of us together, unknown
at the ocean dipping in our toes.

Prayer for the Out

The night, the street – off City Road – the out,
the breath, the dark, the cold,
the smoke, the spliff, the needle, the trick.
Hooker, tart, chastity keeper,
wife and daughter. L.O.L

The car, the bridge – off City Road – the out,
the breath, the dark, the cold,
a railway arch, twenty for oral,
the fish factory cart,
the wheels of a Rover.

A crack pipe first before we go out
in case it happens to be our last
in case he decides to torture us.
The night, the wind, the sleet, the cold,
bad weather brings them out.

Out girl, bad girl, wrap me up in duct tape,
squeeze my nipples in a clamp girl –
I'll give you a grand – good money
for the rattling – stab you in the neck
if you're not what I want.

The tops, the tits
but never the lips,

keep the punters at bay.
Time for a fix and a prayer
to the pimp

before we're off down City Road, the out,
the breath, the dark, the cold,
a John, a cuff, a strangulation,
body in a bin bag,
martyr to the cause.

Penitent we come to you,
Our Lady of the Sinners, sisters beaten down,
and raped before us, absolve us
from our shameful secrets,
baptise us on the City Road.

The Comfort of Women

Doves of peace, paper cut,
folded like cranes, we sit
your head resting in my lap

my hand captive
on the cloth of your arm
where hand meets wrist

our arms bare, our thoughts
bare of how we ended here, how
all we have to give each other

are the tracings of before,
names scratched in plaster,
strings hidden in prison

caps, feet bound, we whisper
our illicit lullaby, fly
with the bird of imagination.

You might think we are sleeping
but our thoughts race,
we hear what you say,

what everyone says, about
our worth, our worthlessness
it happens in our heads,

mostly our bodies are dead
but for the forbidden touch
of one on another,

your arm around me
as we walk down B Wing,
in that moment

helpless, fledgling,
wind catching the sun
throwing us up into the trees.

Fight

You don't remember what started it, there in the upstairs classroom with the windows, where you spent your afternoons, backs to the Sewing Workshop, in the insistent, electric hum of next door's machines, women with their heads bent over the mending of men's clothes, looking out over vans coming into the yard, unruly lines of visitors, straggling children, the garden party in their donkey jackets and greens at the flower bed: dig, plant, water, weed, dig.

Most likely what started it, a dig, some snide remark, intentional aside.

There are no girls gardening, none watching and there is no calling it, no playground chant of *fight, fight*. Just a scream as she leaps across the desk. Just a fist, a bomb going off, a blow to the chest. Your palm's sweat, your breath stolen. Someone, not you whose job it is, presses the panic bell, others herd you to the corner. In a matter of seconds officers pile in, attempt to pin down the braying of youth. Hair floats in the storm. Handfuls of peroxide blonde at loose in the air. There is blood on the floor. You watch, skater on the edge of the ice, wondering if it will hold, waiting for the shift. You have never seen a fight like this before, nor the quiver of fear on the lips of the S.O.

When the men arrive, they put an end to it, overpower by numbers and force. The rebels removed, the classroom sighs out. The women ask if you're alright, knowing you were not bred for it. Though you once had a fight and got a fat lip, but it was nothing like this. In the silent drift to the windows you watch the men, shoulders down, laughing, going back across the yard.

The Listening Project

Prison made poets of you – is what you say
in a roundabout conversational way, is implied
by your words: the comics because reading
passed the time, the dreams and wanting to write
it down, your persistence, knocking, knocking
on Education's door, and a young man called Dan
who invited you into his cookery class
and showed you the skills you already had,
the best time of your life until then, you say.
As I listen I'm reminded of that time in Asda
lifting the weekly shop from the trolley onto the
conveyor belt, pleased with the green stuff, the fruit
and veg, a good shop, health, and the checkout girl
looking at me and saying, *You don't remember me
Miss, do you?* And I know she's been in prison and
I know not to say but I don't recognise her face
I don't remember her name. *It's alright, Miss*,
she says as she scans a bag of lettuce,
*but you were the one who taught me to read
and look at me now!* She beams.
I say something like, *that's fantastic.*Meaning
what she's achieved is fantastic, truly.
Meaning teaching someone to read is not a lost
item in a shopping trolley. So how come I'd forgotten?

Tulip Fever

And all the while the women dreaming,
planting by moon in the fallow soil of night
red tulips for cutting cups
galleries of crystal vase, sapphire
lamps, pearl ash leavening

what every prisoner knows:
we make our prison
according to the season;
Ahmet Altan in his cell in Silviri,
waking to the whisper of snow,

taking tea with Dr Zhivago
in that dacha with the front room window,
three by three, never alone
he eases through walls,
on the swallow's wing

of endless mind, walks unseen.
Without birds, the garden a prison yard,
without tulips, no fever,
no growing rain falling like silk
on the hollow stem of drought.

Asylum

Online Etymology Dictionary – *early 15c., earlier asile (late 14c.), "place of refuge, sanctuary," from Latin asylum "sanctuary," from Greek asylon "refuge, fenced territory," noun use of neuter of asylos "inviolable, safe from violence," especially of persons seeking protection...*

All that remains turning to leaf,
the tenderness of green outgrows brick.
Leaves unfold across a continent of walls,
paint peels and rust blooms on the unhinged,
netted, gates.

In the Tin House: boxes, boilers, chamber pots.
In the Sewing Room: sewing machines.
In the Morgue a trolley the colour
of a bird's egg, embalming table, rubber hose,
overhead lamp, poised.

On the floor newspaper. Mice nest here,
in the home of the incurables.
The first, Mary Rote, arriving by boat at Ovid's
Landing came in chains, others chicken-crated,
naked, fed through holes, disembarked

to a paradise of fields, high-ceilinged rooms.
How light it must have been with such windows,
greeting the sky – all of it,
walking in the gardens by the lake.
In the basement a bowling alley.

In the eaves: A-frame timbers the colour
of beeswax, and a hundred or more
brown leather suitcases lit by the afternoon sun,
sorted in racks, treasure
packed in hope,

brought, stored, long forgotten,
dusted off, opened and catalogued
with an all-seeing lens.
What remains slowly turning to leaf,
grieving late the unlearned lessons.

Frank C

Brimming with photographs:
a breed of smiles and clasped hands,
women in fur coats and heels. In the middle
the frowning child in knitted hat,
peering ahead to abandonment.

Anna

If you die here, they will place your unclaimed ashes
in an urn and keep your suitcase for posterity.

Not that you knew to begin with, only what you
brought and how hard it was to remember.

Now you roam the walls, dance at the windows
of the beauty salon, keep your toothbrush in its rack

wear the gowns, yoked and colour coded: red
for danger, blue for melancholia, yellow for mania

and the straitjacket with ringed holes, placket
and string, for those wild times when the lake calls.

Thelma R

You didn't pack a dress,
only small china dogs, a primer on race,
The Secret Place,
and your *Christian Philosophy of Life*.

At the chair by the window in the hall
paint peels like a jigsaw, you rub a flake
with your finger, green the colour
of underwater inhabits your nails.

You keep your mind on squares and checks,
bible and ruler. Small, dark, I picture you,
too much life, strutting, passerine,
screaming jay.

You didn't pack a dress,
just a pair of pink ceramic lovers
and your All-Star Decca Record, Tony Martin's,
I Guess I'll Have to Dream the Rest.

SILENCE

Silence

When something bad happens in prison it hangs in the silence and in the absence of movement. The prison is locked down. The corridors are empty. There are no prisoners milling about, coming back from breakfast or dinner, joining queues for medication, and the staff are all cloistered in offices and on the wings. All the usual markers of the day are gone, and for a time the prison becomes a ghost of itself.

I wasn't in the prison the day Lisa hanged herself from her cell pipes. She did it in the early evening, with a ligature made from her bedsheets. Sadly, when they cut her down it was too late. I took the phone call at home. The Principal Officer on the wing, who was a good friend, called to tell me. He and I had talked often about Lisa. We knew her well. I was not only her teacher but at her request and his I was helping Lisa to write down and explore her life story. Now she was gone, her young life wasted. Was it really what she'd intended?

Lisa's death wrapped itself around us like a shroud, heavy with questions, weighted with loss. It is hard to quantify the loss and the guilt that comes with a death in custody. The whole prison, from the Number One Governor down, mourns. The prison feels its failure.

The day or night slows down into a numbness punctuated by quiet exchanges between staff trying to ascertain exactly what happened and who was involved. Such postmortems on the facts stretch into the days ahead. I remember worrying a great deal about the work I'd been doing with Lisa and what impact that might have had. I also remember us all being puzzled and fooled by her cheerfulness in the preceding days. I remember too, feeling relieved that I had not been the one to open the cell door and find her. Ultimately, I was very grateful to be well received by Lisa's family at her funeral.

Lisa was larger than life, always at your door pestering you but in a way that was endearing and irresistible. She was well liked among staff and prisoners. She was very young, just nineteen. The night I learned of her death I dreamed of her. I dreamed I was choking and fighting for my breath. The nightmare woke me.

It was hard to go in through the gate the next day but I was met outside by a fellow teacher who came in with me. Most of all I wanted to go to the classroom, even though I wasn't teaching, just to talk to the women and to share our shock and sorrow. I also saw my friend, the Principal Officer who'd phoned me. I knew he was the person who felt most like I did that morning. Meeting meant we could offer each other some crumbs of comfort.

I was never really in doubt as to why Lisa might want to take her own life. There was no mystery as far as I was concerned. If I'd had to endure what she'd endured as a child, I might have done the same. Some things are impossible to live with because the pain runs too deep. I am not sure that we failed Lisa. She was about to be released and that can be a very difficult time for a woman who has valued the safety of prison. I do not think she took her life because prison was a tough and uncaring environment. I do not think it was what we did to her that caused her suicide. At least I hope it wasn't.

I experienced this kind of silence, the kind weighted with tragedy, only once more. It was on the occasion of the death in custody of a newly arrived prisoner on the Induction Wing. Very few of us outside of the wing knew this young woman but we were all saddened by her death.

At the inquest into Lisa's death, those of us who were called to appear waited outside the Coroner's Court. We sat brooding, with little to say to one other, except to offer our support as we each returned from giving our evidence. We were lost in our own thoughts, remembering Lisa and wondering what else we could or should have done.

This silence, the kind that eats the air and hangs over you like a swollen rain cloud sucking the breath out of the day, also hung over the prison hospital. This was where the most distressed prisoners, the sick and those with the most serious mental health problems were lodged. There were occasional outbursts of howling and crying out, of kicking off, smashing up – the sounds of prisoners losing control – but otherwise it was a mute, isolated place where women were locked into the silence of swallowed words and griefs. It was a place apart from the rest of the prison.

In the old Female Wing, the hospital mainly held prisoners on a murder charge who were not allowed to mix with others. I entered this hushed, scrubbed and disinfected world with caution and trepidation. The sister in charge was formidable. The sound I best remember from the hospital corridor was the soft squeaking of her crepe-soled shoes on the floor. The women I visited there, to offer cell-studies, were charged with killing their partners or their children. I don't ever remember meeting a woman who'd killed a stranger. Occasionally there were women in serious need of psychiatric care who could not survive on the residential wing.

There were only one or two women in the hospital at any time. Their lives were solitary and highly controlled, but they were not locked up for twenty-three hours a day as prisoners in segregation were, and in the new prison the hospital was less isolated, busier, though still very separate. As I experienced them, prison hospitals were a law unto themselves. They operated independently, had a reputation for prescribing paracetamol for everything, and also sadly, for neglect. In the early days, I worried that someone might actually die from lack of treatment and I know the Board of Visitors shared my concerns.

All prisons have a Segregation Unit, sometimes called the block, a unit for the control of prisoners who are considered to be a danger to others or to themselves. The purpose of the Seg, as it was called, was to provide a cooling off period. It was never intended for long term use, though in some prisons or with certain prisoners it was and still is used as a permanent solution. Low Newton did not rely heavily on the segregation of prisoners. Other units I visited in other goals were far worse. But with its tomb like concrete cells, the banging shut and locking of heavy, reinforced, steel doors and its lack of any simple comfort or any visual stimulation, it was still a place of social isolation, inactivity and control which I found deeply disturbing.

It seems to me barbaric to keep anyone in segregation for more than a few hours – even those prisoners who might request it, as some do, wanting to get away from the wings. As for keeping a prisoner in Deep Custody, as it's officially called, for years, I cannot find an explanation for this erasing of a soul. The vast majority of prisoners held in segregation have serious mental health needs, yet segregation has been found to lead to increased anxiety, depression, anger, difficulty in concentration, insomnia and an increased risk of self-harm. Which of us could survive well in these conditions?

I have always had an interest in the provision of care for the mentally ill and in the history of asylums. I grew up around a mother who suffered with serious depression and who, after a failed suicide attempt, only narrowly escaped admission to hospital herself. I also worked for a time as a volunteer in an old psychiatric hospital on the outskirts of Norwich city, the kind of hospital that was closed in the 1980s. In the prison I sometimes wondered how much we'd learned since the days of the old asylums. Standing in the doorway of a segregation cell, looking in on a forlorn, depressed woman, a woman whose fight had gone, whose anger had most likely been swallowed up and internalised to be taken out on herself in an act of self-harm, you could be forgiven for thinking that little had changed. That this, in fact, was worse.

I'm not sure that any good ever comes of solitary confinement and I worry about those who advocate its use and who enjoy the power it bestows. Here is Nelson Mandela:

'I found solitary confinement the most forbidding aspect of prison life. There is no end and no beginning; there is only one's mind, which can begin to play tricks. Was that a dream or did it really happen? One begins to question everything.'

The Fifth Labour

You thought you knew how they felt
when the van came into holding in the yard,
how they felt when the gate closed
behind them, hidden in their horse box stalls,
windows black as muck from the Augean stables
and no river running through,
when the automatic gate failed, exposing them
to the world, women made naked in their dreams.

You also dreaded the unseen,
corridors, cornered spaces and the weight of iron.
Dreaded being found wanting in impossible Herculean
tasks – brokering power, staunching pain –
the worst of it when she twisted sheet to rope
and hanged herself on the pipes.

Someone had to meet you outside the gate
that morning and take you in
because that's what you did for each other.
And you went to the P.O.'s office on a new wing
and the boss put his arms around you and
told you he knew how it felt.

Mary Oliver Says – You do not have to be good

I wish I'd known her poem then,
known more confidently myself,
our bird-dog steps
the schlep of our worlds.

I would have shared it with you,
given it you to read, copy by hand,
decorate with roses or vine
or ways of your choosing,
stick with toothpaste
on your own empty noticeboard
with the corners torn and missing.
Better still graffitied it across the walls
of your cell
YOU DO NOT HAVE TO BE GOOD

You did not have to cut yourself with broken
biro casings, push staples under skin,
kneel to scrub, tie a ligature to the bed.
You did not have to be his repository,
barrel, firkin, vat, vessel,
nor apologise to me for the hustle.

You did not even have to make an application
You only had to be *the soft animal of your body*

and what it loves...tell me about despair,
yours, and I will tell you mine.

We Are All Made of Stars

Through the Galilee Chapel,
stone and glass, to the smallness
of being in this place,
in the last bay of the nave
before the crossing
I light a candle – a tea-light for 50p.
As the flame takes, imagine her freed
flying on supernova wings
to begin again in another body
half-formed of atoms from beyond
the Milky Way
in her own funny galaxy.

At work, I say – *I lit a candle,*
it was all I could think to do.
You say – it gets to you when there's
trouble and non-believers like me
light candles in cathedrals.

At the inquest

we sat in an overheated lobby
with plastic plants and vending machines,
drinking coffee, waiting to be called,

retreating to the dusty crawl
space of thought, scuttling like cockroaches,
antennae out – our *should haves*,

our, *did what I coulds, more than I should,*
our, *couldn't have knowns, she drove me mad
but, wish I listened, called, been curious,*

*checked up, deemed it serious, got there
sooner, hadn't panicked, understood,*
feelers poking up through the boards

preparing to colonise the house, shedding
skin on polished floors, feeding on the dried
milk at the sleeping baby's mouth.

In a Painting by Vermeer

It was my birthday when we met, both barely
out of childhood. I didn't have keys.
Sister unlocked you for me. I thought it strange,
in the hospital they liked to keep their prisoners
apart, restrained. You were in strips,
a mattress on the floor for fear of distress,
crouched in canvas I saw your wound.
Light drew bruise, pinned sapphires in your hair,
a girl in a painting by Vermeer.
I clothed you in weld, turban of ultramarine
silk and a single pearl drop earring.
Sister shot the bolt.

I knelt beside you, your crime hung between us,
an underpainting bone black, you whispered,
He's dead. I killed him.
The police came twice but did nothing.
I was only trying to defend myself.
How can I ever forgive myself?
I sat with your tears that fell like the rain
on the wild green earth above my house.
Sister returned. I'd nothing to offer
but a book and to say I'd be back.

Now, we are so much older and I'm ashamed
I don't remember what you got,

though I think it was two for manslaughter.
Today another birthday, I carry you with me
to the wilds above my house.
No longer crouching or kneeling, we walk
following the silver skein of path
through meadow grass, cuckoo spit, rattle, clover.
Comfrey and vetch poultice our wounds.
We take off our turbans,
let the morning wind free in our hair.

Infanticide

Something Red

Something red, blind flesh
I'd got used to who I was – used

then you arrived flaccid, loose,
purple bruise

and with his nose. I no longer
knew who I was – and you –

you were something red
that cried, whose crying

refused all soothing. I knew
I was not the one

to bear child; who I was
could not bring her

into the world, while staying
true to my mirror-self.

Pillow

The label reads hollow
fibre stuffing, in other words

poly-fill dirt cheap, easy
to clean, a short life span

no feather or down requiring
constant fluffing, no shredded

memory foam, memory intact
as you press down. *Shush*,

as the pillow escapes its slip
catching breath like smoke

in a cup, cupping nose and
mouth in the white unsullied

cotton of relief. *Shush,
Shush*. It happens with ease,

the clump of it under your hands,
pressing down.

And when they know,
when you come to confess, you will

tell how he was lurking,
how it could only worsen in time,

and the articulated, jacked-up truck
of it pressing into your chest,

the concrete pillow, will lift
and you will find peace.

Questions

murmurings
at your parted lips, you sit

on the edge of the bed,
plump, inert, nothing in your cell

but a plastic cup on the
locker top and a copy

of Woman's Weekly
window onto brick.

I stand in the doorway,
it's as if you don't see me,

as if time lodged

between us must first

be coughed up. I try not to think
about what they're saying

out there in the red-top world:
the charge, your infamy.

I step inside. Look for contact
of eyes through pebble glass.

Your feet are small.
Your shoes neat, laces-ups.

You wear a mother's skirt,
but you are young

to have had so many children
and watched them die.

I sit beside you on the bed,
offer books. You do not lift

your head or speak, a trace
of smile anoints your lips, you nod

into yourself, mother I see you
are good at playing child, as if

it's a place you might return to
and start over. I try not to think

of innocence or guilt, how long
you will have contemplated

killing or how, if that's what you did.
Sister says they're watching you

for fear of what you might do
to yourself, it will help if you're occupied.

I hand you a pen, an exercise book,
and wonder how alone you are.

Where is he in all of this?
Where your mother?

Where the whispering neighbours
who tried to run you out of your house,

who said you never cried?
And us, where are we in all of this?

In the Segregation Unit

I ask to see you,
they look at me like I've got religion
or some unwanted disease.
Still after all these years they refuse
to believe I am not one of them.

You want to go in there, see her?
You want me to unlock that door?

Yes. Please.

There are no mango trees in segregation,
no limbs growing into each other
grafted on,
there is only separation
alone

you raise your eyes to greet me
then down at the cardboard potty on
the concrete floor, down
to your fancy dress strip-gown.
You cannot offer me a bed to sit on
or tea or mango juice.

There is only stone and the window so
high we might as well be far out in deep

space, the caged light our spaceship,
with its film of dead, black flies.

Stone Dress

Any imposition of solitary confinement beyond 15 days constitutes torture.
Juan E. Méndez, United Nations

Her body is covered with a skin as hard as rock
they sometimes call her Stone-Dress.

The sharp finger of her right hand is spear, the knife
she uses to dissect herself.

They keep her behind doors in the petrified forest
of the inhuman, unfit,

left to rot, thin mattress on a concrete platform
steel toilet, colourless brick.

They keep her in Deep Custody, but for an hour
or less a day in the yard

high-wired and featureless, a rhomboid sky.
Out here her weapon leaves no scar,

out here she builds bridges in air, mountain
pansies bloom in the small cleft of her, clinging

like alpines to rock. Her dress folds to spindrift.
If she could, she would lie on her back and hum

at the hidden stars. Five years she has lived like this,
Stone Dress, scaring the birds from the forest.

Agnes Richter's jacket

Agnes Richter (1844–1918) was a seamstress who is remembered for an embroidered jacket she made whilst held in Heidelberg psychiatric hospital.

In Heidelberg at the close of the century,
pen and paper forbidden,
you embroider your resistance,
words and numbers, yours in red repeated
583m, 583m, a number, no longer Agnes,
delusional so father, so brothers said.

You say: *I am not big, I wish to read, I am his, I carry,*
no cherries, inform me, happiness, I have not been confirmed.

Your words shape
the framed existence,
like music on a stave,
equation, line, couplet,
your garment page,
pleated at the shoulder
leg-of-mutton sleeve
flared cuff, seven buttonholes.

You wear your bodice inside out,
tricky to read, skin tight,
coarse institutional linen, brown wool collar
stained with sweat, ragged hem
and you a seamstress by trade
perhaps why they allowed you the
troubling of a uniform

some might call art –
a *Drowning Dress*,
silk and cotton floss, lead fishing weights,
after Virginia Woolf,
a Tracy Emin quilt –
some might call craft
some asylum
after a mad mother's fine coats and dresses.
My mother was also a seamstress, Agnes Richter,
stabbing the needle in the jacket tattoo
inked on *Ich*
the contours and creases of being
crumpled like paper in a wastepaper bin.

WINDOWS AND GATES

Windows and Gates

In the prison there was barely a view of the outside world. Views were nearly all concrete, brick and yard. Windows were barred, small, and sometimes high up. There was little that resembled glass; panes were narrow, cloudy and set in reinforced pre-cast stone. At one time I worked for over a year in an office that had no window at all, and my previous office in the Education Department was perpetually dark, despite its meagre window. Mostly my working life inside the prison was spent under artificial strip lighting.

So perhaps it's no surprise that I have a thing about windows. Among my favourite paintings of all time are the paintings of open windows by the French painters Matisse, Bonnard and Dufy. In these paintings, colour and light pour in, blue skies and water call to freedom, to the outside world and the poetry of the landscape. The view entices you from beyond the room as no view in prison ever can.

Windows, view and light are just some of the reasons I love my house so much, modest though it is. It's built on an east west axis. I can stand in the bay window at the front and look out at open fields, then turn and look all the way through the house to the small glass conservatory at the back and the garden beyond. The house is flooded with light, especially in the summer. I cannot imagine working in the prison, as I did, and living in a dark house.

Like the light, the air in prison was recycled and institutionalised. A school dinner smell wafted out of the kitchens and mingled with the scent of human sweat, bleach and blood. Wings were dominated by the aroma of industrial cleaning products with the occasional sweet whiff of Comfort fabric softener. The women bought it in the canteen, diluted it and used it to wash their cell floors. They too were conscious of the air and its smell. When I left the prison in the evenings, as I stepped outside, I would do what many others did – take in a big lungful of air. Outside the prison, the air tasted different.

The main gate was a portal between two worlds. The gatehouse was the liminal space that sat on the boundary between them. On a good day, going in through the gate and collecting your keys was part of the daily ritual of transition, but in difficult or traumatic times, for instance when several teachers ingested L.S.D. from water in the staffroom kettle, somehow tampered with during night classes, and had to be led out of the prison, coming back in through the gate took huge resolve. In problematic situations like this, it was standard practice for people to be met outside and accompanied back in through the gate.

Once I'd left the prison for good it was very hard to imagine going in again.

Finding your way around inside the prison was not difficult because pathways were circumscribed. If you had keys it helped. When I first started teaching, I was not important enough to be issued with keys. If I was going from the male side where the teachers' staffroom was, to the old Female Wing, this meant I had to stand and wait at every internal gate, and believe me there were plenty, for a member of staff to arrive and let me through. At such gates, I received any number of propositions from officers: a drive out, a picnic, a drink, a meal, a look at some etchings – yes, there was humour too – and any number of comments on my appearance. I was fair game, a hostage, just like the prisoners. Those who commented were men used to getting away with that kind of banter. Honestly, sometimes it was OK, but sometimes it wasn't, and I dreaded the arrival of certain of the men.

Once I got keys, it was a huge relief. I could finally make my own way around the prison, locking and unlocking gates. I'm good with keys now; I can get them to work in the most stubborn of locks. Keys were a blessing and a curse because wearing keys clipped on a chain, folded into a pouch on a belt around your waist was not a great look, but it was one I came to accept as part of my ordinary working day, like so many other things over which I had no control or choice. In time, I grew used to the place and it grew used to me. It even sanctioned my going in with flowers.

There are any number of things that you cannot take into prison, in particular anything that might be used as a weapon. There are also many items, like tools, which are strictly controlled inside. Not surprisingly, firearms are on the forbidden list, but a teacher who was once allocated to my class, had managed to smuggle a gun into a high security unit for a prisoner and help him escape (not at Low Newton, I hasten to add). I wasn't sure there was anything I could teach her. Bringing in flowers, as I sometimes did, could hardly be compared with smuggling in a gun.

I brought flowers in for my office and for my classroom to make the place seem more human and to bring light and colour into the day, for myself and for the women, though there was no such thing as a decent vase to put them in, glass being too dangerous. I used old tin vases and have no idea where they came from. I don't know of anybody else who did this but I was considered somewhat eccentric anyway, and I was never once stopped, or my flowers searched.

Thus I would come in, flowers in hand, as the women were coming out of breakfast, cartons of milk and oranges in their hands. At times like these, the central corridor would be like a busy street where we'd meet one another, staff and prisoners, as neighbours and colleagues. And the women would often stop me to chat or ask me for something, or to say hello again, having been out and come back in. I liked the prison at these times, when it was most alive. But I understood that the public thoroughfare of the central corridor was not an easy place for an anxious prisoner, not that they had any choice because this was where they had to queue, in long lines, for medication.

It was the same after lunch, when women drifted in and out of each other's cells or sat on the steps at the end of the wing, blow drying their hair, getting ready for a visit or work, shouting out to one another, singing, noisy. It was a very different, solitary, and more melancholy place at night once the women were in their cells and the prison locked down.

What I missed most when I left was being part of this community. I did not miss the lack of light or view, the stale air or the absence of sky. I missed being known, arriving every day at the gatehouse to collect my keys and hearing my name, and the women knowing me too. I'd become part of the fabric of the place. I could walk through it and see where I'd helped to change it physically, creating new workplaces, a new Library and a Learning Shop for vulnerable prisoners. I missed the people I worked with; the brilliant and dedicated teachers, the prison officers and managers, the activities staff and my lovely admin officer, who kept the world from my door when life was stressful. Prison could be tough and to work there you needed all the help you could get.

I particularly missed the men I worked with. I went back a long way with some of the officers, right back to the early days of the old Wing when their arrival in that all-female kingdom caused more than a stir. The atmosphere changed for ever with their coming and for the better. The women prisoners liked them and found them more fun and much less judgemental, as did I.

One of my great friends in the prison spoke often about the people who were prepared to 'die in the ditch,' for you. It sounded dramatic, I think he enjoyed that, but I knew what he meant; prison could make you very vulnerable, no matter who you were or where you sat in the hierarchy, because there was always the possibility of coming face to face with serious trauma and it was essential to have trusted people around you. Occasionally, only very occasionally at Low Newton, prison was a dangerous place where you needed someone to put themselves on the line for you. In prison, there are acts of bravery that go unheard.

In twenty-five years I was never in any serious danger because I only had to press the alarm bell (the bells were everywhere) and I could taste the adrenalin surge as the officers came racing from every corner. Like all the staff, I had my difficulties with prisoners and with life in general, and it was my friends – the teachers and the good officers of the prison – who baled me out.

Going in With Flowers

Later she went in with flowers, like honey in glass
for the hollow women with little fires in their chest

that refused to be put out, for herself, for the hell
of it, for the green apple stem and earth,

and in the darkness there was colour, small strewn
flags, yellow like morning, red for dusk.

They let them in, clutched unsearched as if a flower
were a holy thing even to them, to a man in black

gloves looking for bombs, opening and closing gates
to the narrow crack, as if flowers were mourning

ghosts falling like rain on every prison's roof.
She took them in, hoping the rain would fall

and every spat word, waiting hurt, every gloss wall,
mirror blurred, every no glass vase

would expand, bloom, transform itself
to dance like wildfire through a burning house.

She took them in because they said what was in
her heart, what could not be said in ink:

it is summer in the mind, cherries are falling
on the grass under branch

this is your house, this is my house,
these our flowers.

What Men Do

I knew a man who swapped himself for a hostage;
brave, when the taker had a degree
in torture and humiliation.
I knew a man who swapped himself for me
when the going was tough, and I was out
with the tide not waving but drowning.
I knew a man who cut a prisoner down – too late.
I knew a man, big as he was, at a loss,
who called me to his office to tell me a woman
had disclosed and him dumbstruck.
I knew a man who liked a tab,
I sometimes scrounged one,
wore his heart on his tie pin, had a sick wife.
the prisoners liked him.
I knew a man unjustly charged.
I knew a man who got what he deserved.
I knew a man wore gold chains under his collar,
like a gangster, the prisoners observed.
I knew a man who let the pain in through his ears
and had to leave.
I knew a man who made us laugh and we were glad.
I knew a man who tried to kiss me in the yard.
I knew a man with a big job and the concentration
of a gnat who put his foot in my hotel bedroom
door and had to be persuaded out.
Who didn't speak to me

at breakfast the next morning.
I knew his boss, a man who rubbed his hands
up and down your back any chance he got.
I knew a man who came to work smelling of gin.
I knew the man who minded him.
I knew a man who wasn't happy about the L.S.D.
in the teacher's staff room kettle,
none who'd had coffee that morning were,
confinement is not good when hallucinating.
I knew a man who was frightened of women.
I knew a man who hated women.
I knew a man who wanted to come to work dressed
as a woman, but as far as H.M.P.S. was concerned
that's not what men did.

How to Spend Twenty-Five Years Inside

Edward Hopper lived on the top floor
of a walk-up with seventy-four steps
and no lift. How he did that
when he got old and his knees rusty

I can't imagine.
But I bet the light up there was wild
Hopper was big on windows.
I'm all over that. I am a Hopper child.

The woman in Cape Cod Morning is leaning
forward into the bay, shutters back,
a stand of trees bathing in morning light,
catching the silvery stretch of it

through cloud, she could be me.
In my house you can stand in a bay
and look through to the back,
glass doors, garden light falling west to east.

Did you know that in Manhattan, twice a year
at the solstice the sun sets in perfect alignment
with the east west streets?
They call it Manhattenhenge.

It matters less on which axis a prison is built
because it doesn't have sufficient
windows to be a portal for light.
Its corridors, wings, gloss walls all tube-lit,

no place for stargazing,
no Atacama Desert, no Yosemite Firefalls.
Prison is no henge,
no compass point, no Aurora,
no artic fox at loose in the sky.

For months on end I would get a headache
every Friday so bad I would have to lie down
in the staff room, drive home blind;
yielding to curtains I grew hollow-eyed,
like the night-diner eluding the day.

How to survive the windowless workplace?
Feng Shui Tips: *grow plants, burn essential
oils, have three different levels of lighting,
white walls, large art, French doors,
frosted glass, a full wall of drapery*

or escape to a house with a bay, where
light comes in like a flood of morning.

Meeting on the Wing

Did you miss me, Miss?
How long have you been away?
You are thinner
your skin grey cloth
rinsed through and shrunk in heroin.

But your cyan eyes still spark wet grass,
peat bog and Burren, Sligo and Down
faraway and out of here
to where we once belonged.

Do flowers miss the sun
and rain?

You know how to spell conflagration
but not how to read.
Perhaps this time
there will be time

What do you think? I say,

girl after my own heart –
I call you girl because
you could be my daughter,
because in here, innocence is all.

Hysteria

We used to laugh – and though I can barely believe
it now – smoke, late on a Friday afternoon
when videos spooled in classrooms
because everyone had Gate Fever,
those who could, already gone,
we'd sit in your office, feet up, coffee,
a packet of fags, headache tablets
between us on the desk and laugh.
Laugh like the girls of the Saltpetriere fed
on chloroform and ether.
Uteruses wandering, we laughed like Charcot's stars.

Marie Blanche Whitman – *Queen of Hysterics*
blond with a lymphatic complexion.
Her skin is white with numerous freckles.
She is very buxom.
Louise Augustine Gleizes – tall and well developed
(buxom, neck a bit thick,
arms and mons pubis covered with hair.)
Were we so different?
Did the girls of the Saltpetriere live among us still?
In the classrooms, on the wings, in rows,
some curtained off: resposantes, incurables.

Few of the patients had been to school,
or knew how to read and write.

The effects of the medication are very marked.
Zinc plates, magnets, ovary compressors, irons
for the cauterisation of the cervix, amyl nitrate,
electrification,
suffering inflicted, enduring,
while we smoked and laughed.
Until it got serious, then we'd discuss
the monthly returns. How many Level Twos,
equivalent to G.C.E in English and Maths,
we could lay claim to,
without being found out.
How many more to reach the K.P.T and be done
with the men gathering at the beds.

K.P.T.s – Key Performance Targets, introduced by
the government

VOICES

Voices

When I think of the prisoners at Low Newton, I barely see their faces; they are shadowy and pale like flowers in a garden at night, bleached of colour. Like a drift of evening primrose, they float ghostly and insubstantial before my eyes. But their voices; their voices sing out. I hear them loud in my ear. I remember their words and I carry them still inside me. Looking back, I see how important those words were, and how the only power the women possessed was voice and the telling of their story.

One of the acknowledged, defining differences between working in a women's and a men's prison is that women want to talk, and talk a lot, whereas men, on the whole are much more silent. Women in prison crave engagement. They want you to know them. They are full of questions, important questions about what is happening to their family outside. If unanswered, as they often are, this causes huge upset and frustration.

Women in prison use their voices to question, protest, kick off, speak out, call out to greet you as the day begins, call to each other, whisper in compassion, laugh and sing. In voice lies identity and power. As Margaret Atwood says, 'A voice is a human gift; it should be cherished and used. Powerlessness and silence, go together.'

Even when I couldn't see the women of Low Newton, when they were behind the door in their cells, or locked up for the night, I would still hear them. Behind the prison mask their voices rose in a company. Like the chorus of a Greek tragedy, they participated in and commented on the drama, refusing to be silenced. Prison has many ways of restraining both those who live there and those who work there. By its closed nature, and with its emphasis on security and secrecy, it attempts to gag. It does not encourage you to speak out or be heard. Those who do are branded as troublemakers or manipulative. In my early days working at Low Newton, when the restraint was greatest, I liked nothing better as I came on the Wing to hear a cleaner, down on her hands and knees, bucket by her side, scrubbing brush in her hand, singing at the top of her voice. Her song would echo off the narrow gloss walls and soar in contradiction. The body might be constrained but the voice was loose and free.

Over time, certain voices became very familiar. These were the voices of the women who returned again and again, the women who worked their way into my heart, whose stories I came to know intimately. For them, prison was a second home. It was a place of safety and they feared returning to the outside world.

Dawn was such a woman; young, child-like and slight, but with a big, beautiful voice, the prison's 'karaoke queen.' I loved to persuade her to sing for me in the classroom, because she had the ability, possessed by all great singers, to lift you up on a song and transport you to another place. The women loved to hear her singing too, and the staff. We kept a bag of make-up for Dawn in the Education Office so that when she came to class, she could put on some lippy and mascara. Along with singing, make-up made her feel good.

On the outside Dawn was a heroin addict and a sex worker. Selling sex financed her drug habit. She often told raunchy tales of life on the street and of her clients, including her favourite George, who liked to put a pinny on and clean her flat. She was up for that any time, she said. Behind the humour and the bravado, behind the make-up and the voice, the reality of her life was grim. It was ruled by her pimp, who kept her mute by beating her up regularly.

It was hard not to take Dawn into my heart, and others like her: Marie who'd been shared between a gang of pedophiles in her family home on a farm, and who'd taken refuge with the pigs hiding and sleeping outside. Mo, sexually abused and starved by her father, who'd foraged in bins to keep her and her sister alive, and who in the end had set fire to her father's house. Sheree, who knew racial discrimination, even in prison, but who sang and clapped the loudest.

It was impossible not to hear the voices of women trafficked across continents, sold to the highest bidders and beaten within an inch of their lives, or the women who lived daily with domestic violence and the threat of losing their homes and their children. And it was hard not to conclude that women in prison were there for the most part because of men.

After a while Dawn stopped coming in and a year later a prisoner told me she had overdosed on heroin and died. I was sad but not surprised. Dawn was typical of so many of the young women in Low Newton, whose lives were dominated by drugs and abusive men. A heroin habit is rarely anything but destructive. Women on heroin would arrive in the prison sallow skinned, stick thin and so sick that I sometimes failed to recognise them. By the time they left they had returned to health. But heroin was never far away. Their dealers and pimps waited for them in the car park or round the corner, armed with that first fix.

I felt the greatest affinity of all with the prisoners of Low Newton. They talked and I listened. We shared our days. If it rained or snowed, we were drawn over to the window together where we would become lost in our own thoughts. We read poetry and stories. I saw their words on the page. We connected. I knew how it felt to carry a lost childhood, as so many of the women did. Many times, I tried to raise my voice on their behalf, to highlight their situation and to argue against the incarceration of women.

The women I met in prison were ordinary women like you and like me 'There but for the grace of God go I.' Ask women in prison what they want and they speak with one voice: a family, a nice house and a car, like you, they say. They want the ordinary decent life that we take for granted. They do not see it as an entitlement, or themselves as worthy. Nor do they make excuses for what they've done or where they are. They take the blame squarely on their shoulders.

The women I met in Low Newton were articulate, funny, kind and wise beyond their years. They were full of bravado, frequently in my face, or in anybody's face. They had little respect for authority or status, including H.R.H. Princess Anne, who visited on more than one occasion. Superficially they seemed intimidating but rarely were. They looked to protect you, not to attack. When voices were raised, they were rarely at me. The voices I heard were sympathetic and kind, and always concerned for my welfare.

I formed strong bonds with many of the women so that they looked out for me when they came back in. They would call out, announcing their arrival, asking for their old job back cleaning the Education

Department, or a place in a certain class. They would ask how I was doing, and offer me their pity because after all, as they loved to remind me, I was still there, doing a much longer sentence than they ever would. It was a joke they enjoyed. The women of Low Newton joked and laughed a lot. Humour was the first line of defence, an essential part of surviving the experience. If the women of Low Newton taught me anything, it was the meaning of survival.

I also learned that if you have a voice, then you must use it. Speak up, and if no one's listening then write your words down. Wendy Robertson, Writer in Residence, taught me the power of my voice and my words. When Low Newton was undergoing change from a men's prison with the small unit for women, to a women only prison, and my expertise was being ignored, she told me to put into writing all that I knew. I did so in a booklet, Working with Women, which was printed and circulated to staff throughout the prison, and later across the female estate. Finally my knowledge of working with women prisoners was recognised. I was consulted about my experience and I was invited to help plan the new regime. My voice was heard, and with it, if indirectly, the voices of the women who have since inspired my poems and these pages.

Now, every time a poem is read, I like to think their voice is heard.

Rain

When it starts up, the women drift to the window,
unfurl in the damp scent of memory, hand to pane,
the sky growing dark, the yard black with rain.

They are seagulls returning to land, wild indigo,
bindweed and clover, turning their petals up
sniffing out the far-off peacock's dance.

They are cows lying down. It is hot inside,
out there cool water drips from posts, clatters off
white vans in the percussion of time when:

of everything left behind, the rarely spoken of,
dangerous to enter unless in disguise,
the who and where caught in rain.

I go over and stand with them, adrift at opaque
squares, smaller than a notebook page, the past
streams from gutters, I am twenty-one, in Paris

for the first time, kicking up leaves in the
Bois de Boulogne, coat at my heels, umbrella blown.
Under the awning of a street café, I write: Dear M,

the journey was fine. Yesterday it rained all day, it rains most days here, but we survive. We watch the rain from windows and think of home.

The Karaoke Queen's survival kit

lived in the stationery cupboard,
back office of the education block
in a plastic crowned H.M.P. bag
smelling of old roses and cheap perfumes.

Your cosmetic lucky dip,
our remnant offerings: foundations, eye shadows,
mascaras and blushers, glosses and lipsticks,
oh, those lipsticks – your street walking,
pay for your wrap, keep the pimp off your back,
red.

Your cock sucking, lip syncing, Amy Winehouse
sing like a demon, *I told you I was trouble,*
you know that I'm no good,
pink.

Morning movement over
classroom doors pulled to
you crossed the central area
like a child alone in the playground
and mouthed at the office window
Can I? Can I Miss?

Pig-Girl

And him a pig farmer. And you his pig-girl,
in the morning out with a bucket of swill
pigwash, mash, all kinds of crap,
they knew, could discern.
Pigs are intelligent, cognitively complex
like dolphins and dogs
loving and capable of suffering.

Your night spent in straw under tin
forbidden as you were to go out:
You dare
You dare defy me
Defy me girl and you'll see.
Come here.

He couldn't find you
out that late in the fields with his torch
out, out shining and blazing,
in the end for once he had to give up.

And you were the rain hard on the corrugation.
You were iron, clatter and sing,
wet snout snuffling, lolling ears
warm spotted skin, softening the fear
that sat in the crease in the arch of your foot,
waiting to jump out.

Wild pig, sow in spate, they bait you
edge away with taunting curled lip:
You dare
You dare defy us
Defy us and you'll see –
until you're wild with it – *fuckendon't care*
with it, *fuckenbastardscrews, fuckeneverything.*

Room spin. Kick off. Pin down. Seg
or a jab in the thigh and a bed in the
hospital where you lie in the sun
snoot to snoot snuff out the buried,
wallow in the coolness of mud.

H.R.H.

She was not in a good mood
by the time she got to us
in the afternoon.

She'd been in Durham that morning
and they'd put her through the search tank
like a commoner, *Empty your bag Mam please*,
note Mam as in Spam, the proper way
to address a royal.

She was flushed,
her handshake loose, indifferent.

In the Art Room you stood up,
I'm Mo, you said,
*doing life for setting fire to me father's house
abused me from a kid he did,
and me sister.
But he's still on the out, and I'm in here,
D'you reckon that's fair, Mam?*

Mam as in Spam was silent
clutching her handbag, as the bodyguards
swooped in and bundled her out,

afraid you might set fire to her
with the torch of your words.

Doing Money

You illegal, he says, *fit for nothing,*
only doing money,
you run, they put you in prison.

Your clothes are hidden, you wear a t-shirt
and briefs, it's cold in the house, mattresses
are damp and soiled, ashtrays stuffed
to overflowing. They come all hours of the day
and night – sometimes in pairs,
sometimes three or more – do as they please
according to cost: to fuck, to cut, to gag
and cuff, tie up, fuckery, sodomy.

Cost more for anal, he says, *more you go bareback.*

There is no charge for burning with cigarettes,
for splitting lips, no charge for the blood that runs,
the bruised head, the cracked nose.
You have no shoes.
Outside the trees are withered and leafless.
The moon is up
a barely seen shadow of itself
it is not the winter moon of home.

You never going back, he says.

There is a hole in you as big as yourself
only your edges are real and your ribbon-less hair.
The shape worn in you is the shape of rock.
Most of you has disappeared
but the girl in the white communion dress visits
your dreams, climbing the steps
cut in your clavicle, parting flesh from bone.
Outside cars wait like crows.

What I Did in the Summer Holidays

You make me sit. *Don't move*, you say
as if I'm your girl. *Yes, like that, lie back,
the body you've got.*

You lean over, the camera eats me,
lens pushing at my forehead,
blood stopped, under my chin

as if to excavate my mouth. *Stick your
tongue out. Bite your lips, loosen
your hair.*

My head is a tethered horse
wanting to run, my lips swell to hooves,
eyes as big as foals.

*Put your arms out. Tits out.
Take off your bra.*
I am young but old,

I am scarecrow, wild service, spindle
in the hedgerow, yearling
foaming at the mouth.

young and wild you build up trust,
allow me to stretch, then harness
and break me in.

Spread your legs. My back bears
the weight of the saddle
my mouth the bridle's steel.

Fully grown, neck down
scuffed and spoiled with mud.
I am your mare, your pin-up.

I am your, *No point in going back
to school, girl,
now you're thirteen.*

Bombing

To tell you the truth – she says – licking her lips grinding her teeth – I can't eat or rest – I'm amped – I'm wide awake on paste – billy whizz-jelly beans – lid poppers – lemon drops – know what I mean – buzzing – to tell the truth – she says dancing around the room on her toes – I love the stuff – can't part with it – gives me a buzz see – have to have it – no not the bumble-bees that goes without saying but the other stuff – the stuff I nick in my shoulder bag – graft – rake off the shelves – bags of it – buzz of it – don't like to part with it – pile it up in black bags – giant cushions – like sofas – it's the comfort – I do it for the comfort see – do it for the ache – and the paper – there's the paper – tell you the truth I like paper too – little squares like this see – keep them in piles all over the house – buzzing – not just black and white I like colours – like I like sparkles and cartwheels – I can do a cartwheel now if you like miss – tell you the truth they all know me in the shops – got my photo up in the back – massive – mug shot see – tell me to leave – get out before they call the cops – get myself worked up – the buzz of the sirens – when they come they know me see – buzzing – I get angry sometimes – tell you the truth – just comes over me – and that's when I put my fist in her face hard – she says.

She hops, darts between desks – didn't they see before they let her out for class? They know her well enough. I know her well enough by now, when she's bombing; the barely drawn breath, rapid fire phatic. Fet, fettle, throttle, the way she pulls up her sleeves to show her arms, skin made of scrape, thin lip of white, razor lines cross hatched, blind, the scars which are nothing – she says – to what's inside. All those blackbirds, black cadillacs, blue boys and brown, funneling through arteries and veins, all that plastic piling up and spilling from her overstuffed house. How to pick up the pulsing, bloodied sac that is her heart lying tremulant at my feet?

Sheree

Because you resist.
Because you are up from the smoke.
Because you taunt them with Holloway
and everything they're not.
Because you are always trading,
hustler in the market of your island home.
Because you know how to slice and peel
a mango, make rice and peas, jerk chicken
on Sundays which the women prefer.
Because you complain at the blood stains
on your mattress and demand something more.
Because you say you will inform the governor.
Because your voice is loud and sweet
and you sing and sway and clap
in the chapel wearing your kitchen whites
despite the chaplain's disapproval.
Because you are fat.
But most of all, because you are black.

Fire

In our house the stairs are steep.
In our house there is a piece of stale cake
in a tin at the back of a cupboard.
Was it a fall, they ask?

In our house a baby was lost.
I looked for her under the bed where knives
were kept. In our house we only eat on Fridays.
Was it a fall, they ask? *Or was she pushed?*

In our house a fridge full of cans
invite you in, come drink
in a house where darkness is wrapped
in blood-soaked rags and swallowed tongues.

In our house sisters sleep in the same bed.
A girl is betrothed to a crow with wings
and a black feathered chest. In our house
we wear our clothes like cloaks.

There is half a sliced loaf in our house
hidden in an Asda carrier in a bottom drawer.
Sometimes Mrs. B brings windfalls,
dry bread and sour apple dull hunger.

In our house an absence of mother.
What happened in our house was night.
What happened in our house turned the blossom
on the cherry red where it was buried.

Was it a fall, they said? In our house I knew
where the matches were kept, newspaper
and paraffin. Fire. Like eating,
it happens so fast we barely taste it.

Remedy for a Small Voice

You saw a picture once of mimulus,
prepared by sun, its roots in stream,
Seep, Sticky, Musk, its speckles reminded
you of your mother's wrist.

You are afraid of the dark, of accidents,
of spiders and birds.
Not a him, but a her, you say
shy, small voice, dread secret

flown up to lodge on the ceiling.
And we who should not be
are shocked. We who swore nothing
could shock, are silent, unfit

as remedy: four drops, four times a day
in a teaspoon of brandy.
There is no rescue from
a mother's freckled wrist

finding its way beneath your sheets,
fingers straying to the hood,
dew on pouched lips, no cure
for the incurable.

Letter to a Prisoner

I'm sorry you're here. Sorry for your loss.
My condolences on the death of a life, for stealing
it from you, making it worse.
I regret you were shipped here like cattle, gold
taken from you, stripped searched, degraded.
I'm sorry the place is colourless and scuffed.
That you must breathe, speak and sleep
at a time that suits us.
That you'll eat where you shit.
You've been through worse, parked in a pram
while your parents shot up, but it's no excuse.
You do not make excuses. I admire that.
My sympathy is with you. I hope you have a friend,
a visitor. I hope you don't have children
or an unforgiving, unrelenting habit
which will destroy pretty much every chance
you have of making it out of here and staying free.
I hope you haven't lost your house.
I'm sorry this might be the only place you've ever
felt safe, that you do not know how it feels
to be home, that you never had a mother.
I'm sorry the cell is bare, the pipes peeling,
that it's either cold or overheating,
that it has no love in, except what you conjure.
I'm sorry the sink is aluminium, furniture bolted
to the floor, windows plastic, unseeing.

I regret that the night is long
and you do not know who will visit or how
you might cower in the corner until morning
comes, making an island of your bed.
I regret the queue for meds is an Ariadne's thread,
that you may never escape the Labyrinth.
I regret the powerlessness, the passivity,
the relinquishing of responsibility, that you cannot
even decide when to make yourself a cup of tea.
I regret we begin to get used to this place,
ease into captivity, that wandering begins
when we are most confined, and all the palaces
of imagination lie beyond these walls.

Duty Governor

Imagine this – evening and the wing locked down,
a bell, red, buzzing, persistent, in the cell
a prisoner collapsed not breathing.
They call for an ambulance, radio for you.

Nurses attempt C.P.R.
When the blue light takes her
she is barely alive. Imagine.

Imagine this – evening and the wing locked down,
a bell, red, buzzing, persistent, in the cell
a prisoner collapsed not breathing.
You call for the ambulance…

a bell, red, buzzing, persistent,
in the cell a prisoner, not breathing.
Imagine.

Imagine this seven times over.
Seven blue lights in and out of gates.
Imagine you imagine the whole wing
going down to a bad bundle,

lethal cut, serial killer,
and you don't know how much.
Imagine seven dead women on your watch.

Key Pouch and Belt

In the beginning I was mad for you, I longed for you
like a prisoner for sentence served,
without you I was nothing, at the mercy of others,
no means of coming or going, partial, hostage
at every barred gate, waiting, wondering
who would come, the price to be exacted.

But once you were mine, pouch in possession,
your arms about my waist, the clutch of you,
I was safe, closeted. Woke with you, dressed
and undressed with you, drove, cooked, kissed
and wrote books with you, shopped, ate, cried,
picked up the kids with you, lay down, drank wine.

I wore you through every season, more than just
an infatuation, no easily discarded lover,
it was the real thing. You counted my heart's beats,
warmed to the heat of my blood. I prised you open
with the deftness of a lover, you clung steadfast
in your devotion, only occasionally spilling over.

There was no stopping us, until that is you began
to fray at the seams, leather creased, pouch undoing,
in need of industrial repair, the weight of you
grown heavy at my waist, my waist grown heavier,
time taking on its new world meaning, desire gone,
on leaving I hand you in at the gate.

LEAVING

Leaving

Coming out of the prison at night, especially in the winter, was when I was most aware of its physical boundaries. The high perimeter fence was lit by eight-metre tall lighting poles which cast an amber glow across the fence and into the no man's land that bordered the prison's margins. The buildings and yards of the prison were similarly illuminated, polluting the night air with their light. The sky was a fog of Sky Glow: the diffuse orange luminance found in urban areas and which hid the four or five thousand stars which should have been visible. I was always glad, after my drive back, to arrive home in the countryside where the stars burned bright.

Leaving the prison, I took a different way out than I did going in. It was easier at night to skirt around the outside of the wings on the paths that separated them from the odd grassy space and the concrete. It meant fewer gates to unlock and lock. At night the prisoners called to each other from their cells and I would hear them as I passed. If I was really late, after an evening class perhaps, it was often a 'Good night, God bless,' that I heard, sometimes directed at me, with a 'Miss,' on the end. Although the interior of the prison was relatively silent at night, especially after lock down, the exterior came alive for a while at least, with the noise of prisoners tapping out messages on the pipes, calling to each other from their cell windows with the latest gossip or the news of the day and passing cigarettes and contraband on makeshift ropes made from sheets by swinging them from one cell to another.

Once the swinging and calling was over, there was the time alone. Sometimes the relief of another day over and the prison mask removed, time to escape into a different space, watch T.V, listen to the outside world, the wind in the trees beyond the boundary fence, a dog barking, the East Coast train. But with the night came danger, the heightened fear, the footsteps on the wing that stopped outside the cell door, the trigger to memory, a flashback to abuse. There was the very real fear of meeting your abuser in your cell at night, something I was told many times by prisoners.

Although night threw the prison boundaries into relief, it blurred the edges of concrete and brick within and made it a more ghostly place. Not that I was ever spooked but throughout the years I heard mention of the prison ghost who lived on the site of the old Female Wing and wandered the hospital corridor. There were officers who refused to go there at night for fear of her, dressed, according to those who had seen her, in her nurse's uniform. I never encountered a ghost in the prison, other than the occasional glimpse of my mother in the medication queue, or in the face of an owl as I came out at dusk.

It was only after I left that I began to question the twenty-five years I spent in prison and how I'd been able to work there in those circumstances for such a long time. When I look back over my own life and childhood, I see that in many ways I was bred for it. As a child, I'd been my mother's carer for a long time and her emotional support from an early age. I understood about depression and I had an inbuilt desire to take away pain and to make things better. There was a sense in which her illness imprisoned me. There were times too when she would lock me away upstairs. I was used to my needs being entirely subservient to others. Nevertheless, despite her own difficulties my mother believed fiercely in the education of women, as did my father, which meant I was also a working-class girl brought up to be keenly aware of the importance of education in enabling women to reach their full potential.

As a child, the out-of-doors called to me and I found my release and joy in the nearby cowslip fields and the river estuary where we played. Yet I spent the majority of my working life locked away. When I finally left the prison after twenty-five years, I was more than ready. It wasn't difficult to leave. I was leaving to start a new life, and to write which I'd become passionate about. I never once regretted my decision or looked back. Neither did I regret the years I'd spent at Low Newton. I could never regret those.

Leaving was exhilarating and for a while I felt like a child playing hooky from school. Being outside during the day, seeing the whole of the sky, tasting the air, had an edge of unreality about it. It was like being on holiday. It was summer when I left. The sun shone, the world glittered, and it was like all those summers you remember from childhood where the weather was perfect. I was free, and until then, I hadn't acknowledged the constraints I'd been under nor the challenges I'd faced going in every day and soaking up the pain that resides in a women's prison.

In leaving I forged a new path and a new life for myself as a writer, but I did not leave the women behind. They are always with me, in my thoughts and in my writing. My fiction is full of women struggling against the odds, helping each other, determined to make something of their lives, like Aiyana in *Sometimes a River Song* who knows she must learn to read in order to survive.

The women of Low Newton taught me to survive. They live in me and in my words. Their voices and the voices of women in prison everywhere are here in these poems. I hope I do them justice.

My Mother the Owl

Gilly-White, Jenny-Owl,
wing feathers the softest of any,
flower-face goddess made of broom,
oak and meadowsweet, the fairest
most beautiful, envied by all.

No builder of nests,
she laid her eggs in the bare places,
timber cavities, tree hollows,
sometimes on the ground in scrapes
of grass and last year's pellets.

At the solstice she floated down
to her mother's house,
gowned in diaphanous white
smelling of French perfume,
perched on the hardwood bed

where her owlets slept
dreaming of dismemberment;
the feeding of one to another
from her night-hunter's hungry beak.
Her breath a sad, eternal frost.

I saw her first on the razor wire,
in the crepuscular hour as I left

the prison for home. After that I found
her daily in the flat, clock faces of
the medication queues, on the wing

in the classrooms, my eyes bathed in
owl feathers ragged as combs.
I could not sleep. I lay awake,
I lay awake on hardwood and frost,
thinking how I'd been bred for this.

And Ghosts Return Gently at Twilight

Slipping through ferrous gates, double-skinned
doors, wings unfolding like an origami bird
paper white, feet first, she comes.
Gone her sensible flat, nurse's shoes,
in their place a pair of Jimmy Choo's,
platinum and flamingo glitter, won
playing poker with the spirits down river.

Our Lady of Shallot trailing bandage and gauze
dripping hem of a uniform
pools into the spareness of our lives,
apothecary to felon, addict, jailbird, pawn.
On her dispensing trolley, tiny glass bottles
like jewels, sapphire and ruby jostle and clink
splintering the night, quieting the wolves

she whispers, *What would you like?*
A Brompton Cocktail, there are worse ways to go
a tincture of morphine, the salve of forgiveness,
a house, a car and two bonny kids?
We admire her shoes, remember who we were,
each her drowned child, each her drowning.
In the morning, a trail of glitter on the hospital
floor.

On a Summer Evening

On a summer evening when the wind ripples
the surface,
those who listen will hear the women talking below,
will hear them whistling and calling from the threes
to the twos,
a set of works dangling at the end of a rope
of clothes,
will hear the London train away on the tracks
a dog barking.
G.B. *God Bless*, knocked out on the pipes,
G.N. *Goodnight,*
in the tap code table, a five by five grid of letters,
co-ordinates tapped out, the night's story unfolding
like a map.
On a summer evening those who care to listen
may hear
the light whispered scuttle of a cockroach on a cell
floor,
the spy flap opening and closing. While those who
care will hear
the ripping of sheets, circling the neck tied to
a bed
the struggle for breath, a slow, hungry asphyxiation,
on an evening when the wind ripples the surface.

In the Night Garden

Let me tell you how night comes
always the same: clock time,
and the prison locked down
the mask unfurled, falling as swollen

leaf to litter, from cracks in the walls
saplings breach the metered space.

You lie on your mattress of maidenhair
a garden besieged

arms sepal, hands palmate
botanical drawing on a page

coloured in flesh and the blooming
of roses from your mouth: *Ophelia,*

Souvenir de la Malmaison.
Incense of nicotiana

and evening primrose drift
through iron bars. In the corridor

the heels of the Night Officer clack
as they pass. The bed takes root

moonlight clatters to the floor.
Outside they are calling

at the windows, their static
infests your Ipomoea ear,

planted when the moon was new
and waxing. You do not sleep

but lie in wait for the whisper
of the night moth's wings.

Sky Glow

It's night when you come out,
put down your bag, unlock the door
the iron gate, pause

look up at the lights on the perimeter
fence scattering dust and gas, through
razor wire, diffuse, luminous

you lock the door
you lock the iron gate, pick up your bag
and make your way to the path

at the back of C and D Wing,
your breath signal out of hiding
caught in the orange light

moth flying blindly for hours
roosting songbird restless in the night,
sky robbed of stars

you round the corner
by the hospital, cells lit, locked down,
that's when you hear her

lone voice across the meagre grass
*Miss what are you doing here, at this time
Miss? You work too hard, Miss.*

She is shadow at the window
mouth to the crack, you wave,
shout, *I'll see you in the morning*,

a morning that will come sooner
than thought, now night is disappearing
and the world lit like never before.

You put down your bag, unlock and lock
the gate by the gym, only two more gates
to the gatehouse, tally and brass,

the handing in of keys,
the out-of-doors, by the time you reach
home there will be trees and stars.

All That's Needed Are Sunglasses

It's hot, July. I wait for you in the Plaza,
exotic beach of white pavers, efflorescent in the sun
at my back the library swells in its glass sea.
People are gathering; alone, together, to drink coffee
under umbrellas, open a laptop, read a book,
get up, sit down as they please, as if everyday.

It's true you can move freely around a prison
if circumstances allow and you are someone
of status, not a prisoner. Someone with keys.
But getting out, leaving
require determination, resilience, immunity to gates.
Now, all that's needed are sunglasses.

So much of a life hidden, we embrace
our fortune like children let out, city girls when
the back of the van opens we run because we can,
no stopping, no road, no wire, no brick-built
obstruction, ill-shod for it in newly borrowed
trainers we fly, our paleness marks us out.

*The temple bell stops but I still hear
the sound coming out of the flowers*
– Basho

Her voice hangs like a bell on my sleeve
sewn to the cuff of my dreams.
Her voice has no influence on weather,
pillow and cloud smothered,
scattered like unearthed bones
dog-nosed, broken china.

Her voice lives in the sea, in the scallop
in the shingle
in the twisted strands of kelp.

Wordless she comes, stealing
my breath, homeless, bed-down
bag and cardboard cover,
her cry snags in the reeds
at the bend of the river on its way
to the cowslip fields.

Language unheard
her voice lives in the earth,
riot of the obstinate, difficult, shy.

An oriole hiding in woods,
woman running with wolves,

perpetual refugee,
her voice is a severed tongue,
hanging on my garden tree.
I hear her still at my kitchen window.

www.ingramcontent.com/pod-product-compliance
Lightning Source LLC
Chambersburg PA
CBHW052206090526
44583CB00017BA/2324